It Starts With A Coin:
The History of Money, for Kids

By Bradley Zink

ISBN: 9798609342492

DEDICATION

I would like to dedicate this book to all of the young readers with an interest in learning the history of different things. To see them enjoy reading, and having the opportunity to learn where everyday things we use come from, is my inspiration for creating fun and informative books, that can be cherished for generations.

CONTENTS

ACKNOWLEDGMENTS

I would like to thank my dear friends in the financial industry, for assisting me in putting this book together. Without their help, this book would not have been possible.

INTRODUCTION

You use it to buy groceries. You use it to pay for the movies, or getting gas. People use money every day, for all sorts of purposes. But, have you ever asked yourself where money comes from or where did money all begin?

In "It Starts With A Coin", we'll take a look at the history of money, from the days of cattle and shells, to the modern day use of electronic money and banking.

So, let's take a brief look at the evolution of money, over the course of human history……

HISTORICAL TIMELINE OF MONEY

9000 - 6000 B.C.: Cattle Cattle, which has included sheep, camels and other livestock, are the 1st and oldest form of money. Once agriculture became prevalent, cultures would barter (trade), using grains and other plant products.

1200 B.C.: Cowrie Shells China was first to use the cowrie shell, a mollusk found in the shallows of the Pacific and Indian Oceans, as a form of currency. Throughout time, many societies have used the cowrie shell for money.

1000 B.C.: First Metal Money and Coins By the end of the Stone Age, China began to produce the earliest forms of metal coins. Made of bronze and copper, and often containing holes so they could be put together like a chain, these metal monies developed into a primitive version of the round coins we use today.

 500 B.C.: Modern Coinage In other parts of the world, coins first developed out of lumps of silver. Over time, these lumps were stamped with images, such as emperors and gods, and took on the more modern-round shape we use today. Unlike the Chinese coins that relied on base metals to produce, these coins used precious metals such as silver, bronze and gold, which had more value.

118 B.C.: Leather Money Leather money was first used in China, made of squares of white deerskin and stamped with colorful borders. These are considered the first type of banknotes in history.

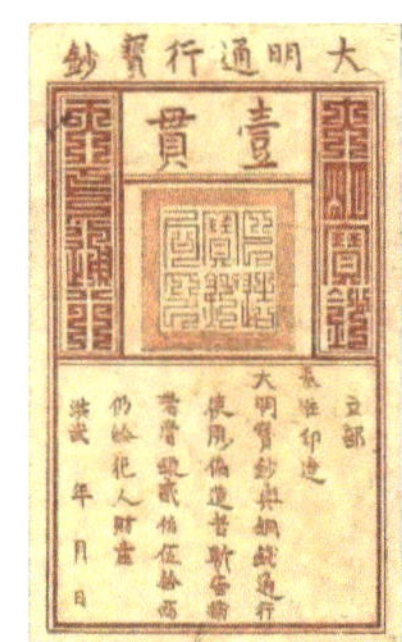

806: Paper Currency Starting in the 9th century, China began to utilize paper to create banknotes. For 500 years, this paper currency was used. Then, with the value rapidly depreciating, paper money disappears from history for several hundred years, reappearing in Europe in the 1600s.

1500: Potlach "Potlach" comes from a Chinook
Indian custom ,existing in many North American
Indian cultures. This was a ceremony where gifts
were exchanged between tribes, along with lavish
feasts and ritual dancing. These exchanges would
not only create a peaceful existence between
tribes, but also established a leader's social rank.

1535: Wampum Wampum, a string of beads
made from clam shells, was used back in the
1500s by many North American Indians.
"Wampum" simply translates to "white",
which was the dominate color of shells used.

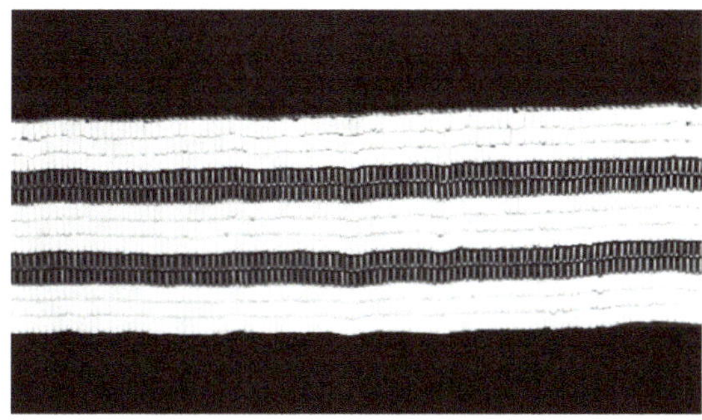

1816: The Gold Standard In the 1800s, England officially made gold the standard of value. Guidelines were made to allow for a non-inflationary production of standard banknotes, which would represent a certain amount of gold. This is the first time that banknotes were tied to gold, thus helping to maintain "value". The United States followed suit, in 1900, which helped lead to the establishment of a central bank.

1930: End of the Gold Standard
The Great Depression of the 1930s, marked the beginning of the end for the gold standard. In the U.S., the gold standard was revised and the price of gold was devalued. Shortly, The British and international gold standards ended as well.

The Present: Today, currency continues to change and develop. More intricate designs and security features, make it harder for modern-day counterfeits to be produced.

The Future: In our modern "digital" age, financial transactions regularly take place electronically. Electronic or "Digital" money, such as Bitcoin, are traded in the form of bits and bytes, and will most likely become the future of all currency, replacing coins and paper money.

HISTORIC TIMELINE OF MONEY IN THE U.S.

1690: Colonial Notes

In the beginning years of our nation, Americans used English, Spanish and French currencies. The Massachusetts Bay Colony issued the 1st paper money in the colonies, that later became the United States.

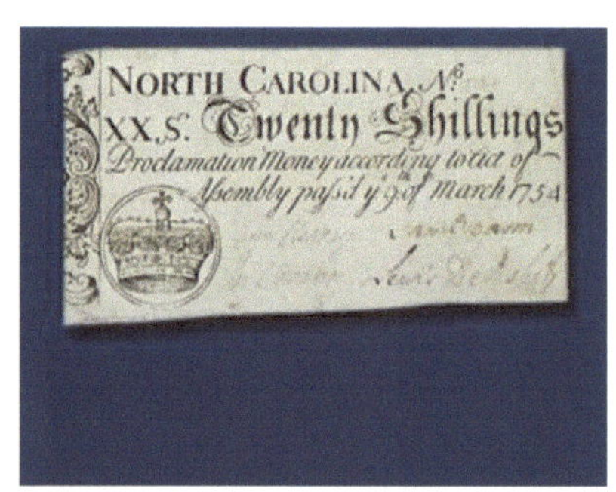

1775: Continental Currency

To help finance the Revolutionary War, the colonists issued paper currency, which were backed by the anticipation of tax revenues. Easily counterfeited, and with no solid backing, the notes quickly became devalued, hence the phrase "not worth a Continental."

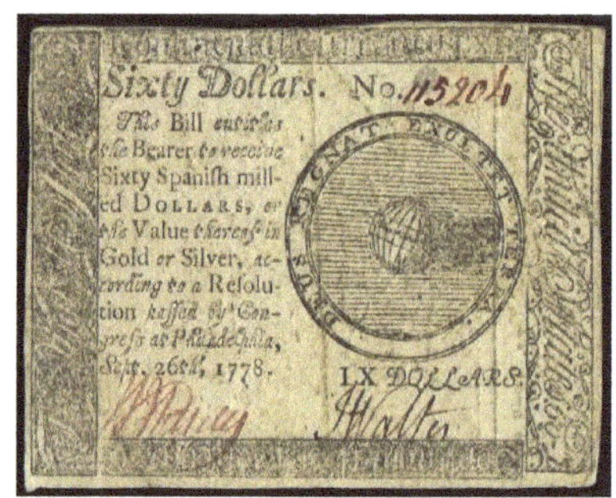

1781: The Nation's First Bank

The Bank of North America, chartered by the Continental Congress, was the nation's first real bank, giving further financial support to the Revolutionary War.

1785: The Dollar

Continental Congress adopts the dollar as the unit for national currency. At that time, privately-owned bank note companies would print a variety of banknotes.

1789: First Bank of the United States

Congress charters the First Bank of the United States. They would authorize them to issue paper bank notes, to help simplify trading and eliminate confusion.

1792: U.S. Mint

With the establishment of the Federal Monetary System, the first U.S. Mint was created. In 1793, the fisrt American coins were struck, in Philidelphia.

1836: State Bank Notes

State bank notes, printed by over 1,600 state-chartered private banks, totaling over 30,000 varieties and colors caused confusion and circulation problems between the States. Also, with so many different 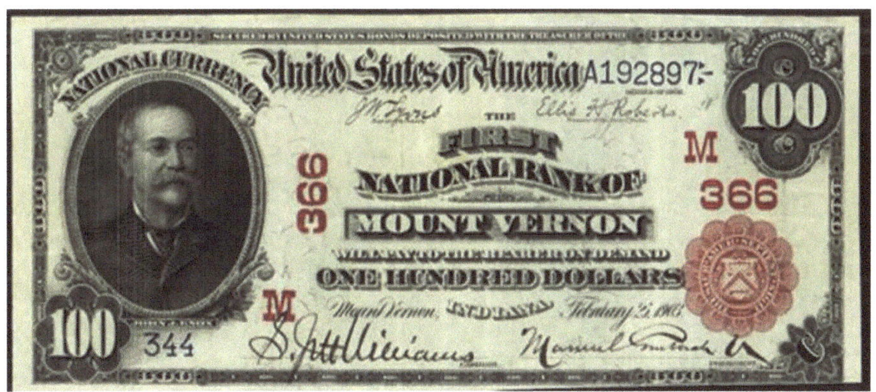 varieties, counterfeiting became an increased problem.

1861: Civil War

Pressed to finance the Civil War, Congress authorized the United States Treasury to issue paper money for the first time in the form of non-interest bearing Treasury Notes called Demand Notes.

1862: Greenbacks

Demand Notes were replaced by United States Notes, commonly called "greenbacks" because of the green tint used, to prevent counterfeiting.. The notes were signed and affixed with seals by six Treasury Department employees.

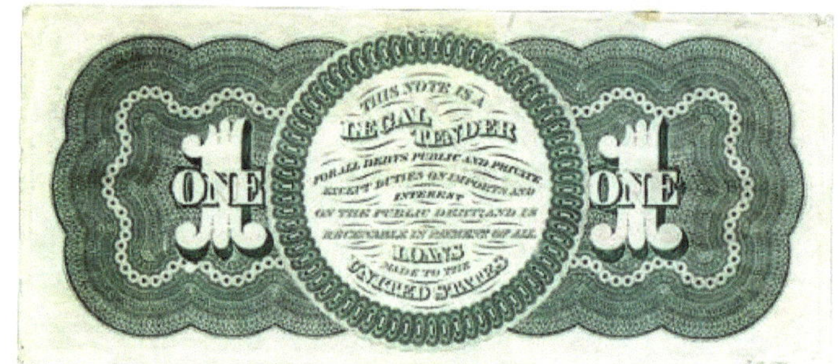

1863: The Design

The design utilized a Treasury Seal, cotton and linen paper with red and blue fibers, as well as fine-line engravings, to make counterfeiting harder to replicate.

1865: Gold Certificates Issued by the Department of the Treasury, gold certificates were issued against gold coin and bullion deposits. These were circulated until 1933.

1866: National Bank Notes

State Bank Notes begin to be replaced by National Bank Notes. Backed by the U.S. Government, this helped stabilize the value of currency, for a short time.

1877: Bureau of Engraving and Printing

The Department of the Treasury's Bureau of Engraving and Printing begins to print all U.S. currency.

1878: Silver Certificates

The Department of the Treasury issues Silver Certificates, in exchange for silver dollars. These were issued until 1957.

1913: Federal Reserve Act

The Federal Reserve Act of 1913 created the Federal Reserve System as the nation's central bank, to regulate the flow of money and credit, for economic growth and stability. The System was authorized to issue Federal Reserve Notes, to become the only U.S. currency to be produced.

1929: Standardized Design

Currency is standardized with a consistent design, with uniform portraits on the front and emblems and monuments on the back.

1957: In God We Trust

The inscription "In God We Trust" is first issued on paper currency. By 1963, all currency was included this inscription.

1990: Security Thread and Microprinting

To continue the fight against counterfeiting, a security thread and microprinting were introduced. 1st featured in 1990 in the $20, $50 and $100 notes, by 1993 the features was included in all notes, except for the $1 note.

1998: 50 State Quarters Program Act

A program that ran from 1999 until 2008, 50 new quarter designs were released, to honor each state's unique history and tradition. The quarters were released, five per year, in the order the states joined the Union.

2000: Redesign of $5 and $10 bills

Again to combat counterfeiting, the U.S. Treasury redesigned the $5 and $10 bills, featuring off-center pictures, watermarks and security threads. From 1996-1998, the $100, $50 and $20 notes also received a similar redesign.

CURRENT PAPER AND COIN MONEY IN THE U.S.

$100 Bill $50 Bill

$20 Bill $10 Bill

$5 Bill $2 Bill

$1 Bill

PENNY

NICKLE

DIME

QUARTER

HALF DOLLAR

DOLLAR

MONEY THROUGHOUT THE WORLD

Chinese Yuan

Indian Rupee

British Pound

Euro

Japanese Yen

New Zealand Dollar

Mexican Peso

Russian Ruble

LEARNING TO COUNT WITH MONEY

Now that we have learned about the history of money and examples of money from the US and around the world, let's have some fun with money counting games. For this section you will either need coins to count, or a piece of paper and a pencil to calculate the answers. To play this game, I will give you an amount and how many coins it takes to get that amount. You have to figure out what coins to use to get the total. (example - $0.26 with two coins = (1) quarter and (1) penny. $0.25 + $0.01 = $0.26). Only use Pennies, Nickels, Dimes and Quarters!

We'll start out with some easy ones, and progressively get more difficult as we go along. Answers to the problems can be found on next page. So, let's begin:

1. $0.27 with three (3) coins
2. $0.41 with four (4) coins
3. $0.56 with four (4) coins
4. $0.82 with six (6) coins
5. $ 0.52 with six (6) coins
6. $ 0.77 with sixteen (16) coins
7. $1.01 with ten (10) coins
8. $1.23 with twelve (12) coins
9. $1.58 with twenty (20) coins
10. $2.41 with sixteen (16) coins

ANSWERS

1. One quarter and two pennies
2. One quarter, one dime, one nickel and one penny
3. Two quarters, one nickel and one penny
4. Three quarters, one nickel and two pennies
5. One quarter, two dimes, one nickel and two pennies
6. One quarter, three dimes, five nickels and seven pennies
7. One quarter, seven dimes, one nickel and one penny
8. Three quarters, three dimes, three nickels and three pennies
9. Four quarters, two dimes, six nickels and eight pennies
10. Seven quarters, five dimes, three nickels and one penny

ABOUT THE AUTHOR

Born in Petaluma, California during the early 1970's, Bradley Zink grew up with a passion for books. Instilled in him by his parents, and surrounded with a library of books by Dr. Seuss, Mark Twain and Charles Dickens, to name a few, he developed a true passion for reading. After the birth of his son, Alex, and being a stay-at-home dad, he too instilled the power of reading in his son. Using Dr. Seuss as the building blocks for teaching him, Bradley aspired to create a book for Alex, and all children to enjoy. With his son as his muse and inspiration, Bradley is constantly testing out his writings on the world's harshest critic, his son Alex.